GROSS THINGS ABOUT YOUR BODY

By John M. Shea

Gareth Stevens
Publishing

Please visit our website, www.garethstevens.com. For a free color catalog of all our high-quality books, call toll free 1-800-542-2595 or fax 1-877-542-2596.

Library of Congress Cataloging-in-Publication Data

Shea, John M.
 Gross things about your body / John M. Shea.
    p. cm. — (Thats gross!)
 Includes index.
 ISBN 978-1-4339-7112-9 (pbk.)
 ISBN 978-1-4339-7113-6 (6-pack)
 ISBN 978-1-4339-7111-2 (library binding)
 1. Human biology—Miscellanea—Juvenile literature. 2. Human body—Miscellanea—Juvenile literature. I. Title.
 QP37.S54 2013
 612—dc23

                                            2011046363

First Edition

Published in 2013 by
Gareth Stevens Publishing
111 East 14th Street, Suite 349
New York, NY 10003

Copyright © 2013 Gareth Stevens Publishing

Designer: Benjamin Gardner
Editor: Therese Shea

Photo credits: Cover, p. 1 (kids) Mlenny Photography/Vetta/Getty Images, (intestine) Steve Gschmeissner/Science Photo Library/Getty Images; p. 5 Anatolly Samara/Shutterstock.com; p. 7 Catalin Petolea/Shutterstock.com; p. 9 Alexander Raths/Shutterstock.com; p. 11 Comstock/© Getty Images/Thinkstock; p. 13 (diagram) MedidcalRF.com/MedidcalRF.com/Getty Images, (magnified intestine) vetpathologist/Shutterstock.com; p. 15 (boy) Jackie Smithson/Shutterstock.com, (magnified skin) Martin Dohrn/Science Photo Library/Getty Images; p. 17 © iStockphoto.com/Rudi Gobbo; p. 19 (girl) iStockphoto/Thinkstock, (blister) ens Stolt/Shutterstock.com; p. 20 © iStockphoto.com/Michael Krinke; p. 21 © iStockphoto.com/Karl Dolenc.

Printed in the United States of America

CPSIA compliance information: Batch #CS12GS: For further information contact Gareth Stevens, New York, New York at 1-800-542-2595.

CONTENTS

Words in the glossary appear in **bold** type the first time they are used in the text.

WE'RE ALL GROSS!

Our bodies are full of gross stuff, but gross isn't necessarily bad. Believe it or not, sometimes our bodies make gross things to keep us from getting sick!

In this book, you'll find out that some gross things about the body, such as bad breath and stinky feet, are caused by **germs**. But others are important to keep your body healthy, such as sweat and earwax. When you learn about them, many of the grossest things about your body are actually amazing!

Germs are always attacking our bodies. Luckily, our bodies work hard to keep us healthy whether we're sleeping, reading a book, or just having fun.

INSIDE YOUR NOSE

Mucus (or "snot") is a sticky, watery **fluid** made in the nose. It helps clean the air you breathe before the air enters your lungs. Dust, germs, and other bits of matter get trapped in the sticky mucus.

Your body makes about 1 quart (946 ml) of mucus a day! You make more when you're sick, have **allergies**, and during cold weather. Most of the mucus flows into the back of your throat, where you swallow it. When dirty mucus dries out, it forms "boogers."

Gross or Cool?

If dust gets in your nose, your body tries to get rid of it with a sneeze. Tiny droplets of mucus leave your nose at speeds of up to 100 miles (161 km) an hour!

When you have a cold, your body makes more mucus to "wash" the germs out of your nose.

7

EARWAX

Earwax, or cerumen (suh-ROO-muhn), is a special oil made by **glands** inside your ears. This oil keeps the inside of your ears from becoming too dry. The sticky oil also traps dirt and **bacteria**, and even slows the growth of bacteria.

New earwax is always being made, so the older earwax travels toward the outside of the ears. There it dries and finally falls out of the ears, along with the dirt and germs it picked up on its way.

Gross or Cool?

Hundreds of years ago, people used earwax to make artwork!

If you're having ear problems, doctors can use special tools to help you. Never put anything inside your ear yourself.

BAD BREATH

Your breath sometimes smells like the food you just ate. Onions, garlic, and cheese have strong odors that stay in your mouth. However, sometimes the bad odor is actually coming from bacteria.

The human mouth is warm, dark, and wet—features that bacteria love! These tiny germs eat small bits of food left in your mouth and then make sulfur, a chemical that smells like rotten eggs. Brushing your teeth and tongue twice a day is the best way to get rid of bacteria.

There are lots of places bacteria can live on the bumpy surface of a tongue.

11

VOMIT

Your stomach is a large muscle. Food enters your stomach and mixes with strong **acids**. The food is broken down in preparation for **digestion** by the small intestine. This is the part of your gut that turns food into **nutrients** your body can use.

Sometimes, your body senses there may be something wrong with food. The food might be spoiled or contain germs. When you vomit, your stomach muscle squeezes tightly to push the food back up and out of your mouth.

Gross or Cool?

Sometimes, your stomach feels upset when your body is confused. This may happen when you're dizzy, traveling, or very nervous.

highly magnified
small intestine

Vomit, or puke, may seem gross,
but it **protects** the body from
dangerous food.

stomach

small
intestine

13

SWEAT

Your body works best at one temperature: 98.6°F (37°C). To keep you cool when you exercise or in hot weather, your brain sends a message to your sweat glands to make sweat, which is mostly water. Sweat glands are all over the body, but some areas, such as the armpits and feet, have many glands.

Sweat travels through holes called pores onto the surface of your skin. As sweat **evaporates** into the air, it cools your body.

Our bodies lose a lot of water when we sweat. That's why it's important to drink plenty of water every day, especially on hot days or during exercise.

magnified sweat beads

DO YOU STINK?

Although they're so tiny you can't see them, bacteria cover your skin! Some of the bacteria are actually helpful. They keep away dangerous bacteria that cause serious **diseases**.

Bacteria are drawn to sweat. Shirts, socks, and shoes keep the sweat on your armpits and feet from evaporating quickly. The more sweaty, dark, and warm these places are, the faster bacteria grow. As they eat dead skin cells and oils, they produce waste containing sulfur, which causes the stink!

Gross or Cool?

In 1 day, a person's foot can produce more than 1/2 pint (237 ml) of sweat!

Bacteria love to live on your feet. The bad smell when you take off your shoes isn't sweat—it's bacteria waste!

BLISTERS

Sometimes when your skin is hurt, its layers separate, and clear fluid flows between them. This forms a bubble called a blister. The fluid protects the skin underneath until the wound heals.

Blisters may be caused by mild burns, including too much sun. Most often, blisters form where skin has been rubbed a lot. You may find a blister on your foot after wearing new shoes. Don't "pop" a blister, or you might give bacteria a way to get inside your body.

Gross or Cool?

A blood blister forms when a blood vessel breaks and blood leaks between the layers of skin.

People can get blisters if they don't wear gloves while using shovels or rakes—or even bikes!

blister

SCABS

You've probably had a few cuts and scrapes. At first, blood oozes from the wound. Special blood cells called platelets, along with other materials, begin to clump and harden, or clot, over the broken skin. This clotted blood, or scab, acts like a **bandage** to stop more blood from leaving the body.

Beneath the scab, the body works hard to make new skin. Scabs also keep disease-causing bacteria out of the body. Never pick at a scab while it's doing its job!

Under a scab, the repairing skin may form a scar. However, scars often fade.

scar

Your Gross, Amazing Body!

Sweating keeps you cool and your body from overheating.

Mucus in your nose helps clean the air going to your lungs.

Earwax keeps your inner ears free from dirt and germs.

Bad breath is caused by bacteria in your mouth.

listers form when skin has een rubbed too hard for oo long.

Your body will vomit if it senses something wrong with your food.

Scabs help stop bleeding and protect new skin.

Stinky body parts are usually caused by bacteria living in warm, dark, and wet places.

GLOSSARY

acid: a liquid that breaks down matter

allergy: an overreaction by the body (including sneezing and watery eyes) to something that isn't usually harmful, such as pollen or pet hair

bacteria: tiny, single-celled organisms. Many kinds are helpful. Some can cause diseases in humans.

bandage: a strip used to cover a wound

digestion: the process of breaking down food into nutrients our bodies can use

disease: illness

evaporate: to change from a liquid into a gas

fluid: liquid

germ: a tiny organism that can cause disease

gland: a body part that produces something needed for a bodily function

nutrient: something your body needs to live and grow

protect: to guard

FOR MORE INFORMATION

Books

Lew, Kristi. *Itch & Ooze: Gross Stuff on Your Skin*. Minneapolis, MN: Millbook Press, 2010.

Macaulay, David. *The Way We Work: Getting to Know the Amazing Human Body*. Boston, MA: Houghton Mifflin, 2008.

Miller, Connie Colwell. *The Pukey Book of Vomit*. Mankato, MN: Capstone Press, 2010.

Websites

How the Body Works
kidshealth.org/kid
Try quizzes and watch videos that make learning about the human body fun.

Your Gross & Cool Body
yucky.discovery.com/flash/body/
Learn more gross things about the human body.

INDEX